DINOSAURS!

UTAHRAPTOR
AND OTHER DINOSAURS AND REPTILES FROM
THE LOWER CRETACEOUS

by
David West

Gareth Stevens
Publishing

Please visit our website, www.garethstevens.com.
For a free color catalog of all our high-quality books,
call toll free 1-800-542-2595 or fax 1-877-542-2596.

Library of Congress Cataloging-in-Publication Data

West, David, 1956-
Utahraptor and other dinosaurs and reptiles from the lower Cretaceous / David West.
p. cm. — (Dinosaurs!)
Includes index.
ISBN 978-1-4339-6725-2 (pbk.)
ISBN 978-1-4339-6726-9 (6-pack)
ISBN 978-1-4339-6723-8 (lib. bdg.)
1. Utahraptor—Juvenile literature. 2. Reptiles, Fossil—Juvenile literature. 3. Paleontology—
Cretaceous—Juvenile literature. I. Title.
QE862.S3W4685 2012
567.9—dc23
2011035921

First Edition

Published in 2012 by
Gareth Stevens Publishing
111 East 14th Street, Suite 349
New York, NY 10003

Copyright © 2012 David West Books

Designed by David West Books

Special thanks to Dr. Ron Blakey for the map on page 4

Printed in China

CPSIA compliance information: Batch #DW12GS: For further information contact Gareth Stevens, New York, New York at 1-800-542-2595.

Contents

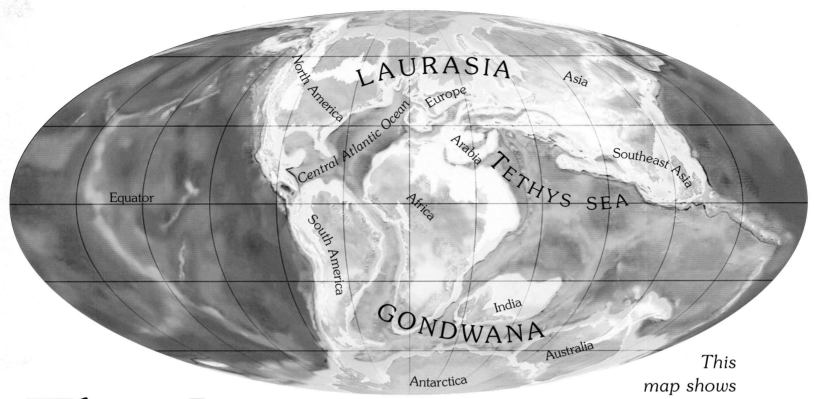

This map shows what the world looked like around 100 million years ago.

The Lower Cretaceous Period

By the end of the Lower Cretaceous period, the continents we know today became more obvious as they split apart from one another. This continued movement of the continents and the rise and fall of sea levels isolated many animals and plants from each other. This led to dinosaurs in different regions **evolving** quite differently. Temperatures on land and sea were generally warm but much cooler at the poles.

*Dinosaurs lived throughout the Mesozoic Era, which is divided into three periods, shown here. It is sometimes called the Age of Reptiles. Dinosaurs first appeared in the Upper Triassic period and died out during a **mass extinction event** 65 million years ago.*

Pterosaurs grew to large sizes.

Ichthyosaurs died out in this period.

LIFE DURING THE LOWER CRETACEOUS

Life in the warm seas continued, with the top **predators**, marine crocodiles, thriving. A few species of ichthyosaurs were present, but they had all died out by the end of this period. Nearly all the dinosaur groups of the Upper Jurassic were still around in the Lower Cretaceous period. Most of the large **sauropods** became smaller, although there were one or two exceptions. **Stegosaurs** became less common and died out, but **ankylosaur** types began to increase. The first frill-necked dinosaurs appeared in Asia. Also appearing in many forms and sizes were dinosaurs with feathers. Evolving alongside were the early birds. Mammals were still small, although the odd badger-sized one **preyed** on small dinosaurs. Flowering plants also began to evolve during this period, and with them, insects and bugs.

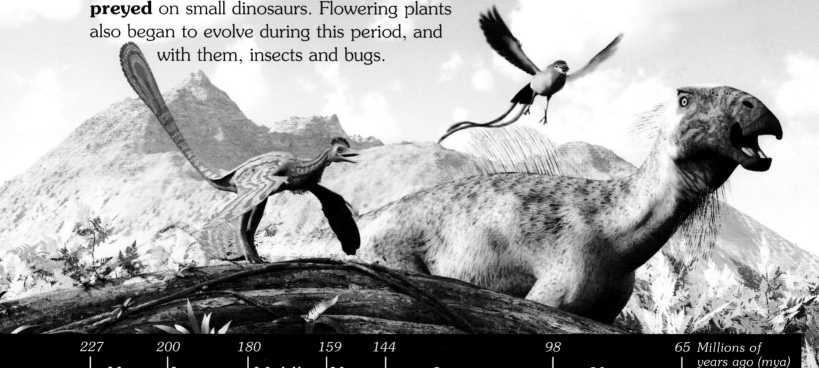

227	200	180	159	144	98	65 Millions of years ago (mya)
Upper	Lower	Middle	Upper	Lower	Upper	
TRIASSIC		JURASSIC		CRETACEOUS		

Giant Sauropods

Fossilized footprints in the state of Texas show evidence of an *Acrocanthosaurus* chasing the sauropod *Sauroposeidon*. These giant sauropods grew up to 98 feet (29.9 m), but the large **carnivores** chasing them grew up to 40 feet (12 m) long and were powerful enough to take on these huge plant eaters.

Paleontologists think that carnivores like *Acrocanthosaurus* would have singled out the weaker members of a sauropod herd, such as

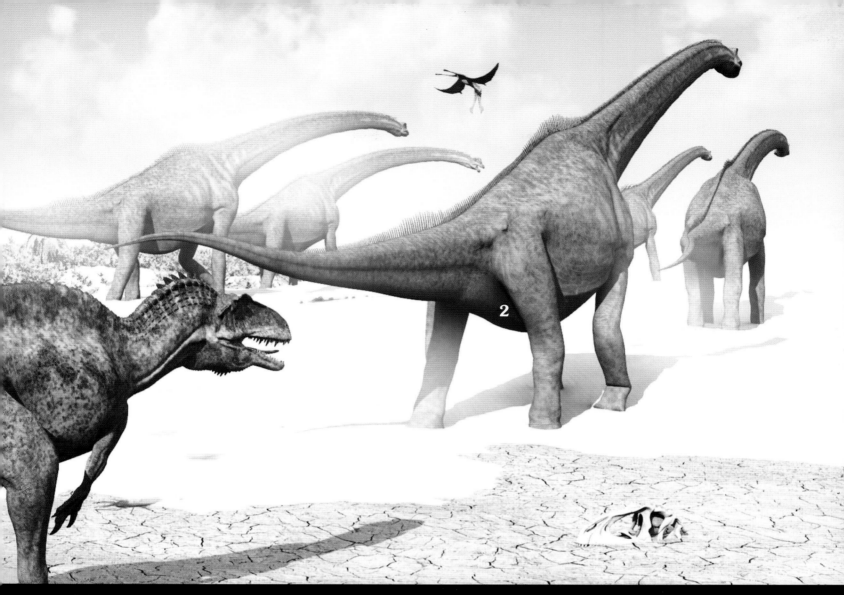

Along a dried-up riverbed, a pair of Acrocanthosauruses (1) *chase after a herd of* Sauroposeidons (2). *They hope to separate a* **juvenile** *from the rest of the herd. In the distance, a* Planicoxa (3) *feeds on a cycad as* Coloborhynchuses (4) *fly overhead.*

juveniles or old and sick adults. *Sauroposeidon* was unusually large for a sauropod at this time, as they were generally getting smaller during the Lower Cretaceous of North America. As well as sauropods like *Sauroposeidon* and *Astrodon*, *Acrocanthosaurus* would have hunted **iguanodonts** such as *Planicoxa* and *Tenontosaurus* (see following pages).

Sauroposeidon grew up to 98 feet (29.9 m) long and weighed around 60 tons (54.4 metric tons).

4

Pack Hunters

Covered in feathers and running in packs, *Deinonychus* was one of the most agile of the North American Lower Cretaceous predators. It was a member of the **raptor** family of dinosaurs, which are noted for the slashing **sickle**-shaped claw on each foot.

These raptors were 13 feet (4 m) long and used their claw to stab and slash their prey, which eventually died from blood loss. To keep the claw sharp, it was lifted off the ground when the raptor ran.

A *heavily armored* Sauropelta (1) *is ignored by a pack of six* Deinonychuses (2) *that are attacking a* Tenontosaurus (3) *on the edge of a giant redwood forest. In the background, an* Astrodon (4) *feeds on the branches of the redwoods.*

Deinonychus was very active and had a large brain for a dinosaur, so paleontologists believe these dinosaurs were warm-blooded. They would have hunted **herbivorous** dinosaurs such as *Tenontosaurus* and *Planicoxa,* and may have attacked the **nodosaurid** *Sauropelta.* This heavily built plant eater was covered in a thick layer of bony body armor, with large spikes sticking out from its neck and shoulders.

Sauropelta grew up to 25 feet (7.6 m) long and weighed around 1.65 tons (1.5 metric tons).

Giant Raptors

One of the largest known raptors lived during the Lower Cretaceous of North America. Its name was *Utahraptor*, and like its relative *Deinonychus*, it was a fast-running and agile dinosaur and may have hunted in packs. It was also probably warm-blooded and covered in feathers.

Roaming the riverbanks and lakesides, this efficient predator would catch prey such as the **therizinosaur** *Falcarius*. This 13-foot (4 m) herbivore

On the edge of a river, a Gastonia (1) waves its tail defensively as a pair of Utahraptors *(2) launch an attack. In the background, a Falcarius (3) is disturbed from feeding by the attack and runs for safety.*

had sickle-like claws on its hands, which it may have used in self-defense. Other plant eaters on *Utahraptor*'s lunch menu were ankylosaurs such as *Hoplitosaurus* and *Gastonia*. These armored dinosaurs were covered in bony spikes from head to tail. Along the tail were sharp, blade-like spikes sticking out from the sides that acted like hedge cutters when the tail flexed from side to side.

Utahraptor grew to 23 feet (7 m) long and weighed up to 1,500 pounds (681 kg).

South America

Wandering the coastal regions of South America was one of the strangest-looking sauropods. Its name was *Amargasaurus*, and it had a row of tall spines rising from its neck and back. These were probably covered with skin, giving it a strange double-hump look.

Scientists are unsure why *Amargasaurus* had this strange arrangement of spines. The skin covering them could have been a way to regulate body temperature, rather like a car's radiator. They were medium-sized

On the edge of an estuary on the coast of Lower Cretaceous South America, a herd of Amargasauruses (1) *flee from an approaching* Tyrannotitan (2). *The herd disturbs a flock of feeding* Tropeognathuses (3) *and* Tapejara (4), *who take to the air.*

sauropods and were likely to have been hunted by large predators such as *Tyrannotitan*. This monster **theropod** grew up to 40 feet (12 m) long and would have had little difficulty catching an *Amargasaurus*. Feeding on the fish along the coast were pterosaurs such as *Tropeognathus* and *Tapejara*. *Tapejara* had a large crest, which was probably colored to attract a mate.

Amargasaurus grew to 39 feet (11.9 m) long and weighed around 8 tons (7.3 metric tons).

Water Hole

Lower Cretaceous Africa was home to a large theropod dinosaur that spent its time fishing in rivers and lakes. This was *Suchomimus,* and its diet was mainly fish and other **aquatic** animals.

Suchomimus's jaws were similar to a crocodile's jaws. Paleontologists believe that although it grew to 36 feet (11 m) long, it probably didn't feed on other dinosaurs unless they were already dead. While hunting along the waterways, it may have come upon *Sarcosuchus.* This giant

14

Searching for fish at a water hole, a Suchomimus (1) *rears back from an attack by a* Sarcosuchus (2). *A group of* Lurdusauruses (3) *look up from feeding, while a herd of* Ouranosauruses (4) *walk past in the distance.*

crocodilian was as long as a bus and may have attacked dinosaurs close to the water's edge. Its prey may have included *Suchomimus, Ouranosaurus,* and *Lurdusaurus. Ouranosaurus* was a strange-looking **hadrosaurid** with back and tail spines that created a sail-like fin. *Lurdusaurus* was a large, heavy plant-eating ornithopod that may have had an aquatic lifestyle similar to hippos today.

Lurdusaurus grew up to 30 feet (9.1 m) long and weighed 6 tons (5.4 metric tons).

Australian Riverside

On a part of the Australian continent of Eastern Gondwana flowed giant rivers amongst creeks, lakes, and swamps. The rivers ran into the Eromanga Sea, an inland sea that was gradually becoming silted up.

Living in and around this water land were a large variety of animals, including **bivalves**, **gastropods**, insects, pterosaurs, turtles, the crocodilian *Isisfordia*, the lungfish *Metaceratodus*, and several types of dinosaurs. One of the largest was a **titanosaurian** sauropod dinosaur

16

A *pair of* Diamantinasauruses (1) *have wandered into a small lake beside a river, upsetting a group of* Isisfordias (2). *One of them has caught a* Metaceratodus (3). *A herd of* Muttaburrasauruses (4) *are on the move, followed by an* Australovenator (5).

called *Diamantinasaurus*. It was an herbivore and had a covering of bony plates. Another herbivorous dinosaur living at this time was *Muttaburrasaurus*. This member of the iguanodontian family had a large, bulging nose that might have been used to produce distinctive calls or for display purposes. Preying on these plant eaters was a large **allosaurid** theropod dinosaur called *Australovenator*.

Diamantinasaurus was 52 feet (15.8 m) long and weighed around 20 tons (18.1 metric tons).

5

1

European Coastline

Fossil evidence shows a huge variety of animals living on the islands of Lower Cretaceous Europe. Among them were small mammals, crocodilians, amphibians, birds, insects, pterosaurs, and a large number of dinosaurs.

If you traveled back 130 million years, you might see a scene close to the sea where sauropods like *Chondrosteosaurus* stripped leaves from trees. Other plant-eating dinosaurs may be feeding close by, such as *Iguanodon*. This well-known ornithopod had a large thumb spike that

A Neovenator (1) *has caught a* Pelecanimimus (2) *as the rest of the pack run for safety. Above them, a* Concornis (3) *flies from a tree. Close by,* Iguanodons (4) *feed on ferns on a hillside overlooking an estuary where a* Chondrosteosaurus (5) *is eating leaves.*

may have been used to defend itself against predators. Along the shoreline, *Pelecanimimus* might be seen stalking fish. This unusual **ornithomimosaur** had many teeth in its beak-like jaws and a small pouch like a pelican. Predators such as *Neovenator* might have hunted these dinosaurs, perhaps watched by one of the early birds, *Concornis*. It is thought they waded along the shore feeding on small **crustaceans**.

Iguanodon was about 29 feet (8.8 m) long and would have weighed around 3.5 tons (3.2 metric tons).

European River

Swamps, lakes, and rivers attracted all types of animals. Apart from fish, amphibians, and reptiles living in the water, animals such as dinosaurs would gather to feed on plants growing on the banks and on the animals in the water and, of course, to drink the water.

Large sauropods like *Aragosaurus* may have found the riverbanks easier to walk along and an ideal feeding area. Other visitors to the riverbank were *Polacanthus*, an early armored, spiked, plant-eating

On a riverbank, an Eotyrannus (1) *chases a group of* Hypsilophodons (2), *who flee to the safety of a pair of* Polacanthuses (3). *Behind them, a* Baryonyx (4) *snatches a fish from the river. On the opposite bank, an* Aragosaurus (5) *towers above the vegetation.*

ankylosaur, and *Hypsilophodon*. Due to its small size, *Hypsilophodon* fed on low-growing vegetation, probably preferring young shoots and roots. A specialist hunter like *Baryonyx* would have spent most of its life by the water, using its curved claws and crocodile-like mouth to catch fish. Predators such as *Eotyrannus* may have made regular visits to the riverside to prey on small herbivores.

Hypsilophodon was about 5.9 feet (1.8 m) long and weighed up to 110 pounds (50 kg).

Scavengers

The rivers of the Cretaceous European islands were liable to flood very quickly. Animals could be caught in the narrow gulleys and drowned before being washed along to the coast. Here they would settle in the silt, providing an easy meal for the many **scavengers**.

A dead *Pelorosaurus* would provide a big meal for many animals. These large sauropods grew to over 50 feet (15.2 m) long. Pterosaurs like *Ornithocheirus* would have been the first scavengers on the scene.

A flock *of* Ornithocheiruses (1) *have been feeding on the carcass of a* Pelorosaurus (2). *They take to the air as three* Concavenators (3) *arrive to feed on the dead sauropod. On the opposite bank, a group of* Valdosauruses (4) *run from the dangerous predators.*

These large flying reptiles rode the air currents over the shallow Tethys Sea, scooping up fish with their sharp-toothed beaks. Predators such as *Concavenator* would certainly have scavenged on dead dinosaurs. These strange-looking theropods had a hump over their hips, but scientists are not sure what it was used for. There is also evidence that they may have had feathers growing from their forearms.

Concavenator grew up to 20 feet (6 m) long and weighed around 2.5 tons (2.3 metric tons).

23

Parrot Lizards

Amongst the cycad forests of Lower Cretaceous Asia
lived a small, gazelle-sized dinosaur called
Psittacosaurus, "Parrot Lizard." It was an early ancestor
of the horned dinosaurs such as *Triceratops*. Fossilized
remains of many species of *Psittacosaurus* have been
found across China and Mongolia.

Psittacosaurus had self-sharpening teeth that were useful for slicing
through tough plant material. However, they did not have teeth

A Psittacosaurus (1) *rears up to protect its young from an inquisitive* Altirhinus (2). *In the foreground, a* Microraptor (3) *chases a* Confuciusornis (4). *In the background, a* Wuerhosaurus (5) *feeds on cycads.*

suitable for chewing. Instead, they used gastroliths, stones swallowed to wear down food as it passed through the digestive system. Living alongside *Psittacosaurus* were herbivorous dinosaurs, such as *Altirhinus* and *Wuerhosaurus*. In the air, birds like *Confuciusornis* were hunted by gliding dinosaurs such as *Microraptor*.

Psittacosaurus was around 5.9 feet (1.8 m) in length and weighed about 44 pounds (20 kg).

25

Asian River Plain

An area of silted-up river plains dotted with lakes and marshes was home to many dinosaurs and other animals from Lower Cretaceous Asia. The climate was **subtropical** and in parts **semiarid**.

Another ancestor to the horned, frilled dinosaurs such as *Triceratops* was present on these flood plains. Its name was *Archaeoceratops,* and it was a two-legged plant eater. It was more lightly built than *Psittacosaurus,* and it had a small, bony frill on the back of its slightly

On a dried-up mud bank, a family of Archaeoceratops (1) *are disturbed by an* Equijubus (2) *as it walks close to their home. In the background, a* Gobititan (3) *feeds on the leaves of trees as* Noripteruses (4) *climb higher into the air on a* **thermal**.

oversized head. Living alongside were larger dinosaurs such as the iguanodonts *Equijubus* and *Probactrosaurus* and the titanosaur *Gobititan*. The air was ruled by pterosaurs such as *Noripterus* and the larger *Dsungaripterus*, which had a wingspan of 9.8 feet (3 m). They used their curved, toothless beaks to prod the shallows of the lakes and riverbanks for crustaceans and shellfish.

Archaeoceratops was only 4.9 feet (1.5 m) long and weighed around 8 pounds (3.6 kg).

Feathered Dinosaurs

Parts of Lower Cretaceous Asia were quite close to the North Pole. In these conifer-dominated landscapes, the climate was cold, with an average temperature of 50° F (10° C). Winters would have been chilly. Many of the dinosaurs living here developed feathers, perhaps as a way of keeping warm in the cold climate.

One of the strangest-looking dinosaurs living here was *Beipiaosaurus*. It was a plant-eating dinosaur of the therizinosaur group. Fossil evidence

Flakes of snow fall on a pine forest as Beipiaosauruses (1) *feed on the low vegetation. A pair of* Sinornithosauruses (2) *squabble over territory, while a* Dilong (3) *chases after two* Caudipteryxes (4). *Above, a lost* Zhenyuanopterus (5) *flies through the trees.*

suggests it was covered in feathers and used its large-clawed hands to dig for roots or to dig out insects from soft wood or earth nests. Other dinosaurs inhabiting the forests include the feathered dinosaurs *Dilong*, a small **tyrannosaurid** dinosaur; *Sinornithosaurus*, a small **dromaeosaurid** dinosaur; and *Caudipteryx*, a genus of peacock-sized theropod dinosaur.

Beipiaosaurus grew up to 6 feet (1.8 m) long and weighed around 187 pounds (85 kg).

Animal Listing

Other dinosaurs and animals that appear in the scenes.

Acrocanthosaurus
(pp. 6–7)
Theropod dinosaur
40 feet (12 m) long
North America

Altirhinus
(pp. 24–25)
Iguanodontid dinosaur
26 feet (8 m) long
Asia

Aragosaurus
(pp. 20–21)
Sauropod dinosaur
59 feet (18 m) long
Europe

Astrodon
(pp. 8–9)
Sauropod dinosaur
49 feet (15 m) long
North America

Australovenator
(pp. 16–17)
Theropod dinosaur
20 feet (6 m) long
Australia

Baryonyx
(pp. 20–21)
Theropod dinosaur
32 feet (9.8 m) long
Europe

Caudipteryx
(pp. 28–29)
Theropod dinosaur
3 feet (0.9 m) long
Asia

Chondrosteosaurus
(pp. 18–19)
Sauropod dinosaur
59 feet (18 m) long
Europe

Coloborhynchus
(pp. 6–7)
Pterosaur
16.5-foot (5 m) ws
North America

Deinonychus
(pp. 8–9)
Dromaeosaurid dinosaur
13 feet (4 m) long
North America

Dilong
(pp. 28–29)
Tyrannosaurid dinosaur
4.9 feet (1.5 m) long
Asia

Eotyrannus
(pp. 20–21)
Tyrannosaurid dinosaur
14.8 feet (4.5 m) long
Europe

Equijubus
(pp. 26–27)
Hadrosaurid dinosaur
23 feet (7 m) long
Asia

Falcarius
(pp. 10–11)
Therizinosaurid
dinosaur
13 feet (4 m) long
North America

Gastonia
(pp. 10–11)
Ankylosaurid dinosaur
19.7 feet (6 m) long
North America

Gobititan
(pp. 26–27)
Titanosaurid dinosaur
Size so far unknown
Asia

Microraptor
(pp. 24–25)
Dromaeosaurid dinosaur
2.6 feet (0.8 m) long
Asia

Muttaburrasaurus
(pp. 16–17)
Iguanodontid dinosaur
29.5 feet (9 m) long
Australia

Neovenator
(pp. 18–19)
Allosaurid dinosaur
24.6 feet (7.5 m) long
Europe

Noripterus
(pp. 26–27)
Pterosaur
5-foot (1.5 m) ws
Asia

Ornithocheirus
(pp. 22–23)
Pterosaur
8.2-foot (2.5 m) ws
Europe, South America

Ouranosaurus
(pp. 14–15)
Hadrosaurid dinosaur
23 feet (7 m) long
Africa

Pelecanimimus
(pp. 18–19)
Ornithomimisaurid
dinosaur
5.9 feet (1.8 m) long
Europe

Pelorosaurus
(pp. 22–23)
Sauropod dinosaur
53 feet (16 m) long
Europe

Planicoxa
(pp. 6–7)
Iguanodontid dinosaur
13 feet (4 m) long
North America

Polacanthus
(pp. 20–21)
Ankylosaurid dinosaur
16.4 feet (5 m) long
Europe

Sarcosuchus
(pp. 14–15)
Crocodilian
40 feet (12 m) long
Africa

Sinornithosaurus
(pp. 28–29)
Dromaeosaurid dinosaur
3 feet (0.9 m) long
Asia

Suchomimus
(pp. 14–15)
Theropod dinosaur
36 feet (11 m) long
Africa

Tapejara
(pp. 12–13)
Pterosaur
16.5-foot (5 m) ws
South America

Tenontosaurus
(pp. 8–9)
Iguanodontid dinosaur
23 feet (7 m) long
North America

Tropeognathus
(pp. 12–13)
Pterosaur
20-foot (6 m) ws
South America

Tyrannotitan
(pp. 12–13)
Theropod dinosaur
40 feet (12 m) long
South America

Valdosaurus
(pp. 22–23)
Iguanodontid dinosaur
10 feet (3 m) long
Europe

Wuerhosaurus
(pp. 24–25)
Stegosaurid dinosaur
26.2 feet (8 m) long
Asia

Glossary

allosaurid A member of the family of medium to large carnivorous theropod dinosaurs that includes *Allosaurus*.

ankylosaur Member of the *Ankylosaurus* family of armored, plant-eating dinosaurs.

aquatic Living in water.

bivalves Aquatic animals that have two hinged shells, such as clams, oysters, mussels, and scallops.

carnivore Meat-eating animal.

crocodilian Group including crocodilians and their extinct relatives.

crustaceans Animals with shells such as crabs, lobsters, crayfish, shrimp, and krill.

dromaeosaurid Small to medium feathered, carnivorous, theropod dinosaurs.

evolving Developing over generations.

fossilized The remains of living things that have turned to rock.

gastropods Snails and slugs.

hadrosaurid Duck-billed dinosaurs.

herbivorous Plant-eating.

ichthyosaur Sea reptile resembling a dolphin.

iguanodonts Members of the *Iguanodon* family of plant-eating dinosaurs.

juvenile An individual that has not yet reached its adult form.

mass extinction event A large-scale disappearance of species of animals and plants in a relatively short period of time.

nodosaurids Four-legged, armored dinosaurs similar to ankylosaurs.

ornithomimisaurs Theropod dinosaurs that looked like modern ostriches.

paleontologist A scientist who studies the forms of life that existed in earlier geological periods by looking at fossils.

predator An animal that hunts and kills animals for food.

preyed Hunted.

pterosaur A flying reptile.

raptor Bird-like, carnivorous dinosaurs with large, scythe-like claws on their feet.

sauropod A member of a group of plant-eating dinosaurs that had very long necks.

scavengers Carnivorous animals that feed on the already-dead corpses of animals.

semiarid An area of very little rainfall that can still support some plant life.

sickle A curve-bladed cutting tool.

stegosaur A member of a group of herbivorous dinosaurs with plates and spikes along their back and tail.

subtropical A climate that has hot, humid summers and mild to cool winters.

therizinosaur A member of the theropod dinosaurs that had long, clawed hands and ate plants as well as small animals.

thermal A column of warm air rising from a sun-heated hot patch on the ground.

theropod A member of a two-legged dinosaur family that included most of the giant carnivorous dinosaurs.

titanosaurian A member of a group of sauropod dinosaurs that includes some of the heaviest animals ever to walk on land.

tyrannosaurid Member of the *Tyrannosaurus* family of carnivorous theropod dinosaurs.

Index